Bye Baby Bunting

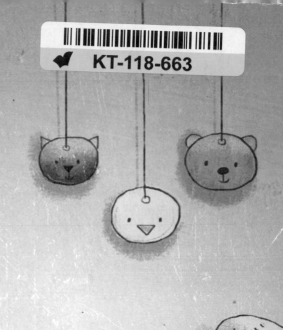

Bye baby bunting,

Daddy's gone a-hunting,

To get a little rabbit-skin,

To wrap his little baby in.

Rock-a-Bye Baby

Rock-a-bye baby,

On the tree-top.

When the wind blows

The cradle will rock.

When the bough breaks
The cradle will fall.
Down will come baby,
Cradle and all.

Twinkle, Twinkle, Little Star

Twinkle, twinkle, little star,

How I wonder what you are.

Up above the world so high,

Like a diamond in the sky.

When the blazing sun is gone,
When he nothing shines upon,
Then you show your little light,
Twinkle, twinkle, all the night.

Then the traveller in the dark,

Thanks you for your tiny spark.

He could not see which way to go,

If you did not twinkle so.

In the dark blue sky you keep,

And often through my curtains peep.

For you never shut your eye,

Till the sun is in the sky.

Star Light, Star Bright

Star light, star bright,
First star I see tonight.
I wish I may, I wish I might,
Have the wish I wish tonight.

Hush Little Baby

Hush, little baby, don't say a word,

Papa's going to buy you a mocking bird.

If that mocking bird won't sing,

Papa's going to buy you a diamond ring.

If that diamond ring turns to brass,

Papa's going to buy you a looking-glass.

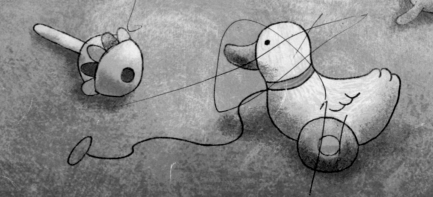

If that looking-glass gets broke,
Papa's going to buy you a billy-goat.
If that billy-goat runs away,
Papa's going to buy you another today.

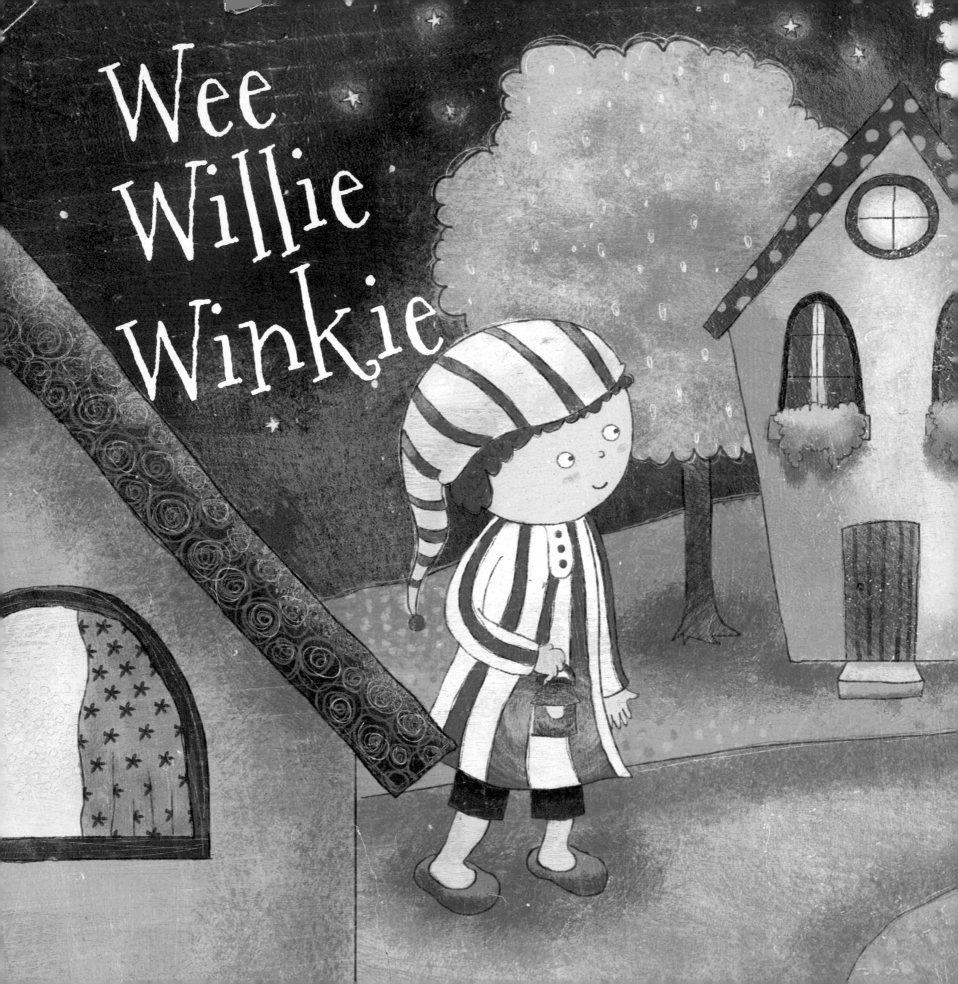

Wee Willie Winkie

Runs through the town,

Upstairs and downstairs

In his nightgown.

Rapping at the window,

Crying through the lock,

"Are the children in their beds,

For now it's eight o'clock?"

Sleep, Baby, Sleep

Sleep, baby sleep,
Father guards the sheep,
Mother shakes the dreamland tree
And from it fall sweet dreams for thee,
Sleep, baby sleep.

Sleep, baby sleep,
Our cottage vale is deep,
The little lamb is on the green,
The woolly fleece so soft and clean
Sleep, baby sleep.

Sleep, baby sleep,
Down where the woodbines creep,
Be always like the lamb so mild,
A kind and sweet and gentle child,
Sleep, baby sleep.

Teddy Bear, Teddy Bear

Teddy bear, teddy bear, touch the ground.

Teddy bear, teddy bear, turn around.

Teddy bear, teddy bear, show your shoe.

Teddy bear, teddy bear, that will do.

Teddy bear, teddy bear, run upstairs.

Teddy bear, teddy bear, say your prayers.

Teddy bear, teddy bear, blow out the light.

Teddy bear, teddy bear,

Say GOODNIGHT.

A Candle, a Candle

A candle, a candle to light me to bed,
A pillow, a pillow to tuck up my head.
The moon is as sleepy as sleepy can be,
The stars are all pointing their fingers at me.

And Missus Hop-Robin, way up in her nest,
Is rocking her tired little babies to rest.
So give me a blanket to tuck up my toes,
And a little soft pillow to snuggle my nose.

Diddle Diddle Dumpling

Diddle diddle dumpling,
My son John,
Went to bed
With his trousers on.
One shoe off,
And one shoe on,

Diddle diddle dumpling,

My son John.

The Evening is Coming

The evening is coming,
The sun sinks to rest,
The birds are all flying
Straight home to the nest.

"Caw," says the crow
As he flies overhead,
"It's time little children
Were going to bed!"

The Man in the Moon

The man in the moon
Looked out of the moon,
And this is what he said,
"Tis time that now I'm getting up,
All babies went to bed."

The End